CLIMATE CHANGE
Simple things you can do
to make a difference

Climate Change

Simple things you can do to make a difference

JON CLIFT & AMANDA CUTHBERT

Chelsea Green Publishing Company
White River Junction, Vermont

First published in 2008 by Green Books, Foxhole, Dartington, Totnes, Devon
TQ9 6EB, UK (www.greenbooks.co.uk)

First Chelsea Green printing February, 2009

Printed in Canada

Text printed on 100-percent postconsumer-waste recycled paper

10 9 8 7 6 5 4 3 2 1   09 10 11 12 13

DISCLAIMER: The advice in this book is believed to be correct at the time of
printing, but the authors and publishers accept no liability for actions inspired
by this book.

Library of Congress Cataloging-in-Publication Data
Clift, Jon.
  Climate change : simple things you can do to make a difference / Jon Clift &
Amanda Cuthbert.
    p. cm.
  ISBN 978-1-60358-106-6
  1. Climatic changes. I. Cuthbert, Amanda. II. Title.

  QC981.C5C55 2008
  640--dc22

                                        2008053491

Chelsea Green Publishing Company
P.O. Box 428
White River Junction, VT 05001
(802) 295-6300
www.chelseagreen.com

CONTENTS

Introduction

INTRODUCTION

What is climate change?

"Climate change" is the changing of the world's climate as a result of what we, the humans on this planet, are doing.

It's a massive problem, and in many people's eyes the single biggest problem ever to face humankind; because if we carry on behaving as we're doing now, we face large rises in global temperatures and also in sea levels, which will have disastrous consequences.

There's plenty we can all do to slow it down. Yes, it is a massive challenge, and a topic that's surrounded by loads of gloom and doom, but fortunately we still have time.

This is not one of those scare stories that pop up now and again in the papers — this is real. So much so that ever since 1988 the United Nations has had a team of about 3,000 scientists from all over the world monitoring what is happening, researching what to do about it, and advising the world's governments.

"Climate change" and "global warming" both refer to the same thing, although "climate change" is a better description because the warming up of the earth changes our whole climate, including how much it rains, the strength of the wind, when and how much it snows, and the frequency and strength of storms.

What causes it?

The main cause of climate change is carbon dioxide, a gas that is produced whenever we burn fossil fuels like oil (in the form of gasoline or diesel), natural gas, or coal. We use these fuels to give us the energy that we need every day. Power plants burn fuel to make electricity for our homes. We burn fossil fuels to move our cars, buses, trains, and planes, to warm our houses, to manufacture our goods — the list is virtually endless.

When fossil fuels are burned, carbon dioxide (CO_2) goes into the atmosphere where, as we burn more and more fossil fuels to feed our ever-increasing demand for energy, the amount of CO_2 gas increases. CO_2 has always been in the atmosphere, trapping just enough heat for life on earth. Now the excess of CO_2 has upset this delicate balance, and not enough heat can escape back into space.

Consequently the temperature of our world is slowly but surely rising, and will continue to do so unless we do something about it.

According to the Energy Information Agency (EIA), our homes produce 21% of the total of U.S. CO_2 emissions, behind the transportation (33%) and industrial (28%) sectors and ahead of the commercial (18%) sector.

What proof is there?

We have all been experiencing more extremes of weather recently. Ever since the world's scientists realized that the world was warming, they have been monitoring what has been going on, and the proof is now staring us in the face:

- The average surface temperature of the earth, together with air and sea temperatures, is rising. We can see this because glaciers are retreating, and in some cases disappearing altogether.

- The ice caps at the North and South Poles are melting.

- Snow and ice, which for millennia has covered large areas of frozen land, is now rapidly melting.

- Eleven of the last twelve years have been the warmest years ever since records were kept.

- Storms and floods are increasing in intensity and ferocity, with disastrous consequences. Weather patterns are much less predictable than they used to be.

- Flowers are blooming earlier, and some migratory birds have stopped flying toward the tropics in the wintertime.

How will climate change affect me?

The world's scientists predict that, unless we dramatically reduce our CO_2 emissions, the temperature of the earth will spiral out of control. This is not going to happen overnight, but things could change far more rapidly than many people expect. The pleasant notion that our winters will just become milder and our summers a little warmer is, unfortunately, not what is in the cards.

Summer temperatures will continue to rise, becoming life-threatening at times. Seriously heavy rainfall and consequently extensive flooding is also expected. Flooding and storm damage will also become more frequent in coastal communities, as sea levels rise and storms increase in ferocity.

In the longer term, as the ice sheets continue to melt, we could face large sea-level rises. The ice sheets melting on Greenland alone will probably raise sea levels anywhere from 19 to 23 feet, with obvious huge repercussions for many cities and areas by or near the coast.

Water supplies will be under duress, with water shortages becoming acute in some parts of the world. This lack of water to both drink and grow crops will, combined with the flooding, create food shortages and force people to move. Large-scale migration is expected, placing huge social and political pressure on the host countries.

With the ice melting and the sea warming, sea levels are rising at a rate of about 3 millimeters (0.1 inch) a year.

What can I do about it?

Now for the good news — there's lots you can do

Most of the world's climate scientists believe we have time to prevent climate change spiraling out of control if we act now. Within the next ten years we all need to dramatically reduce our CO_2 emissions in order to minimize the impact of climate change. It won't be easy — we will need to change our lifestyles — but it is very achievable. Little things that we can do every day can produce large results.

> *Our electricity consumption has gone up 70% since 1970.*

If we all turned off our TVs and other gadgets that are kept on standby, for example, we could shut down seventeen power plants in the U.S., with huge reductions in CO_2 emissions.

We are all using more and more energy: keeping our houses so hot that we walk around in short sleeves in the winter, driving the car just around the corner to get the Sunday paper, popping on a plane for a long weekend abroad in the sun, buying grapes in January that have been flown in from Chile — the list is endless. We need to be more efficient in the way we use energy.

Simple actions can considerably reduce our energy consumption and our energy bills, and help reduce climate change: the less energy we use, the less CO_2 is released, which benefits us all. Once we are aware of what's happening, most of the things we need to do are just common sense.

We don't have to shiver in unheated houses with no modern appliances, or sell our cars and go back to horses and carts; we just have to reduce our carbon footprint.

Climate change terms

Carbon footprint

Your carbon footprint is the measure of the amount of carbon dioxide your activities add to the atmosphere. Surprisingly, many items — from apples to cars — can have a carbon footprint too, especially if they have been flown thousands of miles or if energy has been used in their production. Your purchasing choices can make a big difference to your overall carbon footprint.

Carbon offsetting

Can't I simply pay for somebody to plant a few trees to cancel my CO_2 emissions? While in theory this may seem like a good idea, this process, known as "carbon offsetting," is unfortunately not the way out of the problem.

The theory of carbon offsetting is based on the concept of allowing CO_2 to be emitted now, and then reducing it at a later date. Carbon offsetting generally involves paying a company either to invest in renewable energy projects that may reduce CO_2 emissions in the future, or to plant trees that will possibly take CO_2 out of the atmosphere at some future date. But the problem of excess CO_2 is here today: we can't afford to wait, and need to work in the present.

The setting up of these "offsetting" projects creates the perception that we can carry on polluting at the rates we currently do.

HOME HEATING

What does heating my home have to do with climate change?

- When coal, gas, or oil are burned to warm your house, carbon dioxide (CO_2) is emitted into the atmosphere; this is the main cause of climate change.

- Coal, gas, or oil are burned in power plants to produce the electricity used to warm your home.

Less energy used for heating = less CO_2

What can I do about it?

We spend up to one-half of our household energy bills on keeping our homes warm in winter.

NOW ...

- **Take charge of your heating** — how about turning down the thermostat by 2°F — this can reduce your energy consumption by 10%.

- **Turn radiators off or down** in rooms you only use occasionally.

- **Turn down the thermostat** when you are going away; 40°F will prevent pipes from bursting in cold weather.

- **Set the timer for your heating system** to come on about 30 minutes before you get up or come home in the evening, and to go off about half an hour before you leave in the morning or go to bed.

> **WARNING** — If you are elderly or infirm, try to keep your room temperatures at 65°F at least, and your living room and bathroom at about 70°F.

- **Put on more clothes** rather than turning up the heat.

- **Draw curtains over windows at night**: they provide insulation and help to keep the heat in the room. Avoid covering radiators with curtains — they will funnel the heat out through the glass of the windows.

LATER ...

- **Buy weatherstripping** for your doors and windows. It won't cost much and will make a big difference. You may not want to do this in your bathroom or kitchen if you have problems with condensation. Make sure you still have sufficient ventilation.

> **WARNING** — Don't block up air vents or grilles in walls if you have an open gas fire, a boiler with an open flue, or a solid-fuel fire or heater. These need sufficient ventilation to burn properly, as otherwise highly poisonous carbon monoxide gas is released.

- **Stop drafts coming under baseboards or through floorboards** by filling the gaps with strips of wood, cork, or the correct sealant. Make sure you still have sufficient ventilation.

- **Service your boiler regularly** — it will be more efficient and use less energy.

> *If they're not insulated, almost 40% of all the heat used to warm rooms escapes through the walls and roof space.*

- **Insulate your attic**. This is probably one of the simplest and most effective methods of reducing your heat and energy loss. Attic insulation should be a minimum of 12 inches thick (or between R-30 and R-49). You can do it yourself. There are some very user-friendly materials available, but whichever insulation type you choose, protect yourself with appropriate clothing and a face mask. There may be subsidies available to help you pay for the installation.

- **Insulate your walls**. If you have cavity walls, they are easy and quick to insulate, and in most cases it can be done in a day. Solid walls are insulated by placing cladding either inside or outside; it's more complex, but worthwhile, as solid walls lose more heat than cavity walls. There might be subsidies available to help you pay for this.

If you do just one thing:
TURN DOWN YOUR THERMOSTAT

Hot water

HOT WATER

What does my hot water have to do with climate change?

- When you use gas or oil to heat your water, carbon dioxide (CO_2) is produced; this is the main cause of climate change.

- When you use electricity to heat your water, the power plant burned coal, gas, or oil to produce that electricity — emitting CO_2 in the process.

Less energy used for heating water = less CO_2

What can I do about it?

Don't keep your water heater on all the time — it's cheaper and consumes less energy if water is heated only when needed.

NOW . . .

- **Turn down the temperature of your hot water** at the central heating boiler, at the hot water tank (if your water is heated by electricity), or on your instant (tankless) water heater.

- **Don't waste energy heating water** only to have to add cold water so that it is not too hot to use! A temperature of 130°F is ideal.

- **Take a quick shower rather than a bath** — and make sure to install a low-flow shower head for greatly increased savings.

- **Don't leave hot water faucets running** — use the plug.

- **Bathe with a friend** — you'll use less hot water!

LATER . . .

- **Fix leaking hot water faucets** as soon as you can.

- **Buy a timer for your water heater.** Set it so that the water is only heated when you need it.

Water heated by electricity can cost as much as 70¢ an hour. Just turn it on half an hour before you need it — and don't forget to turn it off afterwards!

- **Buy an insulating jacket** if your hot water tank is not insulated. If you have no jacket, about three-quarters of the energy you are buying to heat your hot water is wasted. Insulating jackets are not expensive — buy one that's at least 3 inches thick.

- **Insulate your hot water pipes.** Insulation is cheap and easy to fit: just clip it around your pipes.

If you do just one thing:
KEEP YOUR SHOWERS SHORT

LIGHTING

What does my lighting have to do with climate change?

- When you turn on a light you use electricity from a power plant.

- Currently almost two-thirds of all the electricity generated in the U.S. is produced in power plants that burn gas, oil, and coal to produce that electricity — emitting CO_2 in the process.

Fewer lights on = less CO_2

What can I do about it?

We spend 7% of our electricity bills on lighting.

NOW . . .

- **Get in the habit of turning lights off** when they are not needed.

- **Use natural light** where possible.

Keep fluorescent lights on, or switch them off?

Some people think that keeping fluorescent lights on is cheaper and consumes less electricity than switching them on and off, because to restart these lights uses considerable electricity.

Restarting fluorescent tubes does require some energy, but only very little.

If you're going to be out of the room for more than a couple of minutes, switch them off.

- **Halogen bulbs** consume a little bit less electricity than conventional incandescent bulbs for the same light output, but they generally need to be used in larger numbers because each bulb only lights up a small area, so you may end up using more electricity.

- **Beware of torchiere lamps**: many consume a lot of electricity, using high-wattage bulbs of 300 W or greater — that's the equivalent of over 30 low-energy lightbulbs! Use energy-efficient spotlights instead.

- **Have candlelit suppers**.

Energy-efficient compact fluorescent lightbulbs are cheap to run because they mainly make light rather than heat. 90% of the energy used by traditional bulbs is wasted in producing heat.

LATER ...

- **Buy and install energy-efficient lightbulbs** — they last about 12 times longer than ordinary bulbs and consume about 1/5 of the energy. They come in all shapes and sizes, including spotlights. Many electric utilities and states have discount programs, and some even give compact fluorescent lightbulbs away for free.

If you do just one thing:
CHANGE TO ENERGY-EFFICIENT LIGHTBULBS

Cooking

COOKING

What does my cooking have to do with climate change?

- When you use natural gas or propane to cook with, carbon dioxide (CO_2) is produced; this is the main cause of climate change

- When you use electricity to cook with, the power plant burned coal, gas, or oil to produce that electricity — emitting CO_2 in the process

Less energy used for cooking = less CO_2

What can I do about it?

Stoves are incredibly energy-hungry; an electric stove with everything on uses about 11kWh (about $1.00) an hour.

NOW...

- **Cut food into small pieces before cooking** — it will cook more quickly.

- **Select the correct saucepan size** for the heating element or gas flame.

- **Put a lid on top of the pan** when you can; your meal will cook much more quickly and you won't be wasting energy.

- **Turn down the heat** when a saucepan comes to a boil. You don't need as much heat to keep a pot boiling as you do to get it to boil, and the contents will cook just as quickly.

- **Only use sufficient water to cover vegetables** when cooking them in saucepans.

- **Use a steamer for vegetables** — you can cook two or three vegetables on one element or gas ring.

- **Consider using a pressure cooker** for cooking some foods — it reduces cooking times dramatically.

- **Make one-pot meals** that only need one element or gas ring.

- **Use your oven efficiently** by filling up as much of the space as possible.

- **If you're cooking a meal in the oven**, don't be tempted to keep on opening the oven door to see how it's all going, as you lose a lot of heat doing this.

A convection oven warms up more quickly, distributes the heat more evenly, and uses about 20% less electricity than a conventional oven.

- **Cook two days' meals at once** in the oven and utilize the space. Reheating will use less energy than starting from scratch on day two.

- **Use the grill rather than the oven** when appropriate.

- **Food will cook more quickly on the top shelf** of a non-convection oven — it is much hotter than the bottom.

- **Use an electric kettle** to boil water for cooking.

- **Keep your kettle free of mineral deposits** — it will be more efficient. Fill it with a mixture of 2/3 water and 1/3 vinegar and leave overnight. Rinse it out well, fill it with water, boil the water, and throw it away.

- **Don't overfill an electric kettle**: just put in the amount of water you want, but make sure you cover the element. You'll use less energy, it will cost less, and will come to a boil more quickly.

Electric kettles consume surprisingly large amounts of energy because they are used frequently, generally heat more water than is needed, and have to bring the water up to boiling point — an extremely energy-hungry process.

- **Make toast in a toaster** rather than under the grill if possible.

- **Plan ahead: get ready-made meals out of the freezer** early enough for them to defrost without using energy.

• **If you are in a hurry**, heat or defrost ready-made meals in a microwave rather than a conventional oven.

• **When cooking rice**, turn off the heat 5 minutes before the end of cooking time, keep the lid on, and let it finish cooking in its own steam.

• **Compost all organic food waste** (see page 55).

LATER ...

• **Get a crock pot;** it's a really cheap way of cooking. The crock pot gently simmers away all day, using little more power than a conventional lightbulb.

• **Electric kettles vary in the amount of electricity they consume;** when you need to replace yours, choose one with the minimum energy consumption.

• **When replacing your electric oven,** consider a convection model — they are cheaper to run.

• **Check out microwave ovens** — they consume about 80% less electricity than a conventional oven.

If you do just one thing:
WHEN BOILING WATER
ONLY USE AS MUCH AS YOU NEED

KEEPING THINGS COOL

What do my refrigerator and freezer have to do with climate change?

- Electricity used for refrigeration and air conditioning units comes from power plants, most of which burn coal, gas, or oil to produce it, emitting large quantities of CO_2 in the process.

Less electricity used for refrigeration = less CO_2

What can I do about it?

NOW...

> *Refrigerators and freezers are never turned off — although they may not appear to use much energy, in an average home they can be responsible for up to 1/3 of the total electricity bill.*

- **Wait until hot food has cooled down** before putting it into the refrigerator.
- **Don't keep the refrigerator door open** any longer than necessary.

- **Keep refrigerators and freezers well away from heat sources** such as stoves, dishwashers, and washing machines.

- **If possible, put refrigerators and freezers out of direct sunlight**, as your appliance will use more energy trying to keep cool in the sun.

- **Try to keep your refrigerator and freezer full**; they will use less electricity.

- **Fill any empty spaces in your freezer** with scrunched-up paper or bubble wrap to stop warm air circulating when it is opened.

- **Defrost food** by putting it in the refrigerator the night before you want to use it. This will cool the refrigerator down and reduce its power consumption.

- **Keep the metal grids** (condenser coils) at the back of refrigerators and freezers **clean and dustfree**, and not jammed up against the wall; this allows the air to circulate more easily around them, and makes them more efficient.

- If you have a fitted kitchen with a built-in refrigerator or freezer, **make sure there is ample ventilation** to allow for air circulation around the condenser coils.

A chest freezer uses less electricity than a front-opening model because the cold air doesn't fall out every time the freezer is opened.

- **Defrost the refrigerator and freezer regularly**. If the ice inside gets more than 1/4 inch thick, the appliances become inefficient.

- **Open the windows** instead of using an air-conditioning unit: air-conditioning is extremely energy-hungry.

- **Draw your curtains or blinds in the heat of the day** to keep the sun out, to keep cool.

LATER . . .

- **Check the door seals on your refrigerator and freezer**: shut the door on a dollar bill. If you can pull it out easily, or if your seals are damaged, they need replacing.

- **Consider buying an energy-efficient freezer** to replace an older appliance. You should recover the cost remarkably quickly.

- **If you are replacing your refrigerator**, remember that a new Energy Star–rated refrigerator consumes about 1/3 of the electricity of some of the older models.

- **Fit shutters or awnings on south-facing windows** to keep the sun out on very hot days.

If you do just one thing:

DON'T LEAVE THE REFRIGERATOR DOOR OPEN LONGER THAN NECESSARY

WASHING DISHES

What does washing my dishes have to do with climate change?

- Energy used to run a dishwasher and heat its water comes from power plants that have burned coal, gas, or oil to generate it, producing CO_2 in the process.

- Water companies also use energy to process and supply water to your home.

Less energy used for dishwashing = less CO_2

What can I do about it?

NOW...

If they are full and in economy mode, dishwashers can be more efficient than washing dishes by hand.

- **When washing dishes by hand**, fill a bowl with warm water and a little detergent, washing the "cleaner" items first. Use cold water for rinsing. Don't do the dishes under a running faucet.

- **If you use a dishwasher**, wait until it is full before using it. Don't be tempted by the "half-load" setting, as it is nowhere near as energy-efficient.

- **Wash your pans in the sink** — they take up a lot of room in the dishwasher.

- **Use the "economy" or "eco" setting** if your dishwasher has one; it will use less electricity and take less time.

- **Switch your dishwasher off completely when it has finished** — it is still consuming electricity on standby.

- If you **switch off the machine and open the door** when the dishwasher enters its **"drying phase,"** the dishes will dry naturally, **saving a considerable amount of energy.**

A water-efficient dishwasher will use as little as 4 gallons per wash cycle, compared with some older models that use up to 13 gallons.

LATER ...
- When you buy a new appliance, get an Energy Star–rated energy-efficient model; they cost less to run, save you money, and contribute less to climate change.

If you do just one thing:
AVOID WASHING DISHES UNDER A RUNNING FAUCET

WASHING AND DRYING CLOTHES

What do washing and drying my clothes have to do with climate change?

- Electricity used for washing machines and tumble dryers comes from power plants that have burned coal, gas, or oil to produce it, emitting CO_2 in the process.

- Water companies also use energy to process and supply water to your home.

Less clothes washing and tumble drying = less CO_2

What can I do about it?

NOW . . .

- **Consider washing some clothes less often** (e.g., jeans).

- **Handwash small items** of clothing in a bowl.

- **When washing clothes by hand**, there is no need to have the water hot. Most nongreasy dirt will wash out easily with cold water and detergent. Cold water is fine for rinsing your clothes afterwards.

- **Wait until you've got a full load** before using your washing machine — using the "half load" setting does not save you half the energy, water, or detergent.

Washing clothes at 80°F uses 70% less electricity than a 140°F wash.

- **Use a lower-temperature wash** for clothes that aren't very dirty: for most washes, 80°F is just as good as 140°F.

- **Use the economy setting** where possible.

- **If your machine has a cold-wash option**, try using it for lightly soiled clothing. Most detergents work extremely well at low temperatures.

- **Air-dry your clothes** on clothes racks or lines if possible — tumble dryers are very energy-hungry appliances.

- **If you have to use a tumble dryer**, then spin dry or wring the clothes before putting them in it. Clean out the lint filter every time you use the dryer: this improves the efficiency, and your clothes will dry more quickly.

- **A water-efficient washing machine** will use as little as 12 gallons per wash cycle, compared with some older models that use up to 27 gallons.

- **Switch the dryer off** when it has finished. It consumes almost 40% of the power while on standby!

LATER . . .

- **If you live in a hard-water area**, and if your washing machine has a heating element, mineral deporits on the element will reduce its efficiency. Every couple of months get rid of it by running the machine empty on a wash cycle using 1 cup of white vinegar in the detergent tray. There are also de-scaling tablets available.

Energy-efficient washing machines use about 1/3 less electricity than older machines. The savings will more than cover the price of a new machine.

- **Get an Energy Star–rated energy-efficient model** when you buy a new washing machine. They cost less to run, save you money, and contribute less to climate change.

If you do just one thing:
USE A LOWER TEMPERATURE TO WASH YOUR CLOTHES

ELECTRICAL APPLIANCES AND ELECTRONIC GADGETS

What do my electrical appliances and electronic gadgets have to do with climate change?

- Electricity used to run electrical appliances and gadgets comes from power plants, which have burned coal, gas, or oil to produce it, emitting CO_2 in the process.

- Energy is used to make appliances and gadgets; the more we buy, the more energy is used to make our goods.

Using appliances efficiently and switching them off after use = less CO_2

What can I do about it?

NOW . . .

In a typical U.S. household, up to 20 appliances and gadgets may be drawing power while not in use, making standby power responsible for between 5% and 10% of the total electricity used in some homes.

- **Turn off the chargers** for your cell phone and laptop when not in use.

- **Turn off TVs, radios, stereos, and computers** when not in use.

- **Set your computer to energy-saving mode** so that the screen is switched off if the computer has not been used for more than a few minutes.

- **Don't be fooled by screensavers** — they use as much energy as the normal screen.

- **Set your computer to switch to standby mode** when you aren't going to use it for a while. The power needed to restart is equivalent to the power used in only a few seconds of normal running time.

> *A computer left on overnight uses 1 kWh of electricity; if 1,000 people turned off their computers overnight, they would save 200 tons of CO_2 emissions every year.*

- **Turn your iron off** just before you finish ironing, and use the residual heat for the last few items of clothing.

- **Do a free energy check on your home** by visiting www.1eere.energy.gov/consumer/tips/home_energy.html and following the links to home energy audits. You can reduce your energy consumption, knock hundreds of dollars off your energy bills, and cut down your CO_2 emissions.

- **Use your electricity meter** to see for yourself which appliances use the most electricity: have a look at your meter while somebody else switches on TVs, toasters, tumble dryers, electric space heaters, etc.

Most DVD players, video recorders, and set-top boxes are never turned off. Even in standby mode some consume about 85% of the power that they use when working.

LATER . . .

- **Think about buying a small portable monitor** that shows you how much electricity you are using, how much it is costing, and the CO_2 you are adding to the atmosphere.

- **Buy a steam iron**: although they use slightly more electricity than dry irons, they are more efficient and take less time.

- **When replacing your computer**, compare overall energy use (both running and standby). Check that it has standby or power-down mode. Consider a laptop — they are more energy-efficient.

- Donate your old computer to a charity that renovates and recycles computers: see **www.computerswithcauses.org.**

If you do just one thing:
TURN OFF YOUR TV
WHEN NOT IN USE

Trash

TRASH

What does my trash have to do with climate change?

- Trash that is not recycled goes to landfill sites. Anything that decomposes in landfill sites will produce methane, a greenhouse gas that seeps into the atmosphere and is 21 times more potent than CO_2.

- The more you buy, the more you throw away. The more new products you buy, the more CO_2 is created by the burning of coal, gas, or oil to create energy for the manufacture of those goods.

- Transporting new goods around the world also produces CO_2.

Less trash = less greenhouse gases

What can I do about it?

- **Use your local recycling facility** to recycle anything not collected by your city or town: plastic, cans, glass, newspaper, wood, telephone directories, electronic goods, cardboard, batteries, electrical appliances, and household goods can all be recycled.

- **Sell or donate things to a charity** rather than throwing them away.

Reduce: if you buy less, you will have less trash
Reuse: if you reuse more, you will have less trash
Recycle: if you recycle more, you will have less trash

Batteries

- **Used batteries are hazardous waste** and must not go in a landfill. Find out at your local recycling center how to recycle or dispose of them. Use rechargeable ones where possible.

Cans

Making goods from recycled aluminum uses only 5% of the energy that is used in making new aluminum.

- **Recycling cans saves huge amounts of energy** — be sure to bring them to your local recycling facility.

Cardboard

- **If your city or town has a cardboard-recycling facility**, use it!

Cell phones

In the U.S., over 150 million cell phones are purchased every year, and over 425,000 are thrown away every year.

- **When replacing an old cell phone**, avoid sending it to the landfill — recycle it. Many charities provide postage-paid envelopes for this purpose.

- **If your cell phone stops working, get it repaired.** There are many companies that will repair it at a very reasonable price.

Clothing

- **Don't be a slave to fashion** — the manufacture and transportation of clothing causes CO_2 pollution.
- **Recycle by donating used clothing to your local thrift stores.**

Computers

- **Rather than replacing your computer**, why not save money and upgrade it instead?
- **Give your old computer to a charity**. They will wipe the hard drive clean and donate it to developing countries.
- **If you need to replace your computer**, look for the most energy-efficient model. Laptops are generally more energy-efficient.

Diapers

Fifty million disposable diapers are thrown away every day in the U.S.

- **"Disposable" diapers take hundreds of years to decompose in landfill sites.** Use reusable cloth diapers whenever possible, and pass them on for other babies to use when you have finished with them.

Eyeglasses

- **You can donate your old glasses** to an optician for reuse in developing countries.

Food

- **Buy only what you need**.

- **Avoid "Buy One Get One Free"** unless you can use or freeze the "free" item.

We throw away almost a third of all the food we buy in the U.S.

A 2004 study showed that 40% to 50% of all the food produced in the U.S. is thrown away.

- **Make a list and stick to it** — impulse buying often leads to waste.

- **Plan your shopping** so that you can use food before its "sell by" and "use by" dates, and find ways of using your leftover cooked food.

- **Pre-prepared meals are expensive**, and are the most frequently thrown away items.

Furniture

- **Unwanted furniture can be sold** or donated to your local thrift store.

Glass

- **Glass is a recycling success story**, which gets better and better. It is easy to recycle — either through your recycling program or bottle redemption center.

- **As well as being turned back into new bottles and jars**, glass can be recycled for many other uses, including fiber-glass insulation and filtration material for cleaning water.

Ink cartridges

There are over 300 million inkjet cartridges thrown away every year in the U.S.

- **Consider using remanufactured cartridges**, or getting them refilled.

- **Don't send used cartridges to the landfill** — recycle them through a charity using their postage-paid envelopes.

Packaging

- **Where possible, avoid packaging** — particularly poly-styrene, which almost always ends up in the landfill and is very difficult to recycle.

- **Try to recycle** any packaging you have.

- **Try to avoid pre-packaged food** — buy bulk if possible.

- **Use your own shopping bags**.

Paper

- **Reuse and recycle paper**.

- **Use both sides**.

- **Make a pad from scrap paper**.

- **Reuse envelopes whenever possible** — many charities sell reuse labels.

- **Buy recycled paper goods wherever possible**, including recycled paper towels and toilet tissue.

- **To reduce your junk mail**, register with the National Do Not Mail List, **www.directmail.com**.

Plastic

- **Waste plastic is a major problem** for the environment, with much of it ending up in the landfill. It is derived from oil, and CO_2 is emitted in the manufacturing process.

- **Refuse free plastic bags** — use your own cotton, hemp, or jute bags instead.

Almost 60% of all plastic waste is discarded packaging.

- **Recycle through your city or town**, or at your local recycling center.

- **Reuse plastic bags and recycle where possible** — some stores take them back.

> *Up to two-thirds of the average trash can's contents can be composted.*

Start composting

- **Making compost** lightens your garbage can and keeps it from smelling.

- **If you compost, less food is sent to the landfill**, which in turn means that fewer noxious liquids (leachate) and fewer greenhouse gases — especially methane — are produced.

- **Homemade compost costs nothing** and is great for your garden. Used as mulch, it can reduce the amount of watering you need to do.

- **Try a Bokashi system or a wormery** if you have no garden space:

    A Bokashi system uses bacteria that thrive without air to ferment the material. No unpleasant smells are produced, and it can be placed and used indoors.

    Wormery — this system is great fun, but requires a little more effort. The worms within it need looking after, but it is most rewarding. The worms eat food waste, paper, and cardboard, producing "worm cast-ings," a very valuable plant fertilizer. There are many different types and sources.

- **If you have some garden space**, you can build a simple compost bin with a ring of chicken wire or a sturdier bin with lumber, or purchase any of a wide variety of available models, including

    Tumblers — available online or at garden centers.

    Green Johannas — the "Rolls-Royce" of the plastic compost bin. The manufacturers claim you need no composting experience. www.greenjohanna.se

    New Zealand Box — more traditional wooden slatted boxes seen in many larger gardens. You can make your own or buy them ready-made.

    Digesters such as the "Green Cone" dispose of kitchen waste, but do not produce compost. www.greencone.com

If you do just one thing: RECYCLE YOUR CANS

TRAVEL

What does my travel have to do with climate change?

- CO_2 is produced when gasoline or diesel is used to power a car.

- Transportation accounts for over 33% of CO_2 emissions, more than half of which comes from our cars.

- A journey by air creates about 10 times as much CO_2 as a similar journey by train.

Less driving and flying = less CO_2

What can I do about it?

More than half of all car trips are under 3 miles, which would take about 10 to 15 minutes by bike.

NOW...

- **Combine your activities** so that you reduce your car trips.

- **Get out of your car** and on to a bus, train, or bike.

- **Check out alternatives to your regular car trips** — can you walk or take a bus?

- **Walk or cycle** part or all of the way when you can.

  A fifth of all the cars on the road in the morning are taking children to school.

- **Get the children on bikes or walk with them to school** — avoid the drive to school.

- **Discover local cycle and walking routes**.

  The effect of climate-changing exhaust gases from planes is around 3 times greater than emissions made at ground level.

- **Share your car trip** with someone else.

- **Get together with other parents for a car pool** — cut the number of cars making the trip.

- **Avoid flying** — look for holiday destinations that you can reach by bus or train.

  Your carbon footprint will be about 10 times smaller if you travel by train rather than plane.

LATER . . .

- **Join a car club**.

- **Try to join a car pool or ride-share plan** if you drive to the same place regularly. See **www.rideshare-directory.com** or **www.rideshare.us**.

- **Arrange your work** to allow you to work from home occasionally if you can — even one day a week will dramatically reduce your car trips.

- **Start a ride-share program** at work.

- **Buy the most fuel-efficient car** you can.

If you do just one thing:
REPLACE ONE CAR TRIP A WEEK
WITH A GREENER WAY OF TRAVELING

Certified Organic
Rainbow
Chard
$2.50 bu

Certified Organic
Yellow Wax
Beans
$5.00 lb

Certified Organic
Fava
Beans
$4.00 lb

SHOPPING

What does my shopping have to do with climate change?

- Everything you buy has an effect on your carbon footprint — the amount of CO_2 your lifestyle generates.

- Your choice of household appliances also affects your carbon footprint; some are more energy-efficient than others, both in their manufacture and their use.

- The kind of food and clothing you buy makes a difference. Artificial fertilizers and pesticides, used to grow most food and cotton, are derived from oil and natural gas, and their manufacture is energy-intensive and emits CO_2.

- When you buy anything made of timber from non-sustainable forests there is an additional impact on your carbon footprint. Trees are the "lungs" of our world — they transform CO_2 into oxygen, thereby reducing the amount of CO_2 in the atmosphere.

- The number of miles your goods have traveled to get from their source to your home makes a difference. All else being equal, the greater the distance, the greater the CO_2 emitted, especially if they have been transported by air.

- Shopping trips by car add CO_2 to the atmosphere.

Buying locally produced products = less CO_2

What can I do about it?

NOW . . .

- **Buy locally grown food, in season**, from your local markets and farm stands.

- **Reduce your food miles** — avoid food that has traveled a long way to reach you.

- **Buy organic if possible**: organic food and clothing will have been grown without the use of artificial fertilizers and pesticides.

- **Buy furniture made from natural timber** that has come from a sustainable source. Look for the Forest Stewardship Council (FSC) symbol.

- **Buy the most energy-efficient household appliances**.

- **Shop online** and get your goods delivered.

- **Plan your shopping** so that you do as much in one trip as possible.

- **Use a bike or the bus** for your shopping trips where possible.

- **Share a car** — shop with a friend.

- **Buy secondhand** if you can.

- **Buy goods that will last**.

- **Buy less!**

LATER . . .

- **Start a local food cooperative** — reduce your shopping trips.

- **Grow your own fruit and vegetables** in window boxes, tubs, or your back garden — zero food miles!

- **Establish a community garden** if you want to grow more.

If you do just one thing:
BUY LOCAL

WATER

What does my water have to do with climate change?

- Collecting, treating, and pumping water for use in your home uses energy.

- That energy has been produced in a power plant that burned coal, gas, or oil to produce it, emitting CO_2 in the process.

Less water used = less CO_2

How much water do you use?

Bath	**20 gallons**
5-minute shower (not power shower)	**10 gallons**
5-minute power shower	**24 gallons**
Brushing teeth with tap running	**1.5 gallons/minute**
Brushing teeth with tap off	**1 quart**
One toilet flush	**2.5 gallons**
Other water use (drinking, cooking, etc.)	**6.5 gallons**
Washing machine	**16 gallons**
Dishwasher	**10.5 gallons**
Washing car with bucket	**2.5 gallons**
Hose/sprinkler	**140 gallons/hour**

What can I do about it?

NOW...

We use 70% more water today than we did 40 years ago.

- **Figure out how much water you use**. Can you reduce that amount and save money at the same time?

- **Never leave a faucet running**.

- **Don't keep the faucet running** while brushing your teeth; use a mug of water — a running tap can use as much as 2.5 gallons of water in the time it takes to brush your teeth.

- **Have a shower instead of a bath**. But if you use a power shower, beware: it can use as much water as a bath if you shower for more than five minutes.

- **Fix any leaky faucets**.

One dripping faucet can waste at least 1,500 gallons of water a year.

- **Avoid using sprinklers and garden hoses**, and use a watering can as much as possible — a garden hose or sprinkler can use almost as much water in an hour as an average family of four uses in one day.

- **Collect the water from your roof** in a rain barrel or two.

- **Use a bowl to wash vegetables** or to wash and rinse plates.

- **Use the leftover water** to water your garden or house-plants, provided it is not too soapy.

Overall, only about 3% of the water entering the average home is actually used as drinking water.

- **Store drinking water in a jug in the refrigerator**, rather than waiting for the tap to run cold.

- **Bottled water has to be packaged** and travels many miles. Try chilling tap water in the refrigerator and see if you can taste the difference!

About 95% of the water that gets delivered to our houses goes down the drain.

- **Only use a dishwasher or washing machine** if you have a full load. If you just have a few things to wash, use a bowl.

- **Wash your car at home** with a sponge and bucket, rather than at a car wash.

LATER...

- **Get a dual-flush toilet** that enables you to choose a short flush most of the time, using a large flush only when necessary. Many people in the world exist on 3 gallons of water per day or less — we can use almost that amount in one flush of the toilet!

- **If you have an old toilet**, you can reduce the amount of water it uses by putting a brick in the tank. (Wrap the brick in plastic so it won't disintegrate over time.) There are commercial alternatives available that can save even more water, and some water utilities may provide them for free or at a discount.

> *Over a quarter of all the clean, drinkable water you use in your home is used to flush the toilets.*

- **If you replace a toilet**, choose a low-flow model rather than a full-size toilet; they use a lot less water per flush.

- **Put a gutter and rain barrel** on your greenhouse or garden shed.

- **Install a low-flow showerhead.**

- **Install water-saving faucets**.

- **Use your "gray water"** (waste water from baths, sinks, etc.): attach a hose to your washing-machine outlet pipe and collect the used water when the machine is discharging. If your bath is one or more floors above the garden, collect your used bathwater as well — siphon it into a rain barrel for use on your flowers. "Gray water" can be used to water your garden flowers, but not vegetables as it can contain fecal coliform bacteria, which might cause illness if ingested.

- **Insulate all outside faucets and pipes** to prevent them from freezing and causing burst or leaking pipes.

- **Have a water meter installed** — you will certainly use less water, and installation is free.

- **Install a rainwater collection system**.

If you do just one thing:
TURN OFF THE FAUCET

Gardening

GARDENING

What does my gardening have to do with climate change?

- Using artificial fertilizers and pesticides in your garden increases the amount of CO_2 in the atmosphere. Fertilizers and pesticides are derived from oil, and their manufacture is very energy-intensive.

- Water companies use energy to extract, treat, and pump water to your home. The less water you use, the less energy is used, and therefore less greenhouse gases are produced.

- Watering your garden using municipal water adds to your carbon footprint.

- Both gas-driven and electrical garden implements add CO_2 to the atmosphere, either directly (if gas driven) or indirectly via the power plant.

More rain barrels = less CO_2

What can I do about it?

NOW . . .

- **Go organic** — feed your soil with natural fertilizers, e.g., horse manure or compost.

- **Feed your plants with natural fertilizer**, e.g., seaweed extract.

- **Use natural pest controls**: for example, spray a mixture made with water and an eco-friendly dishwashing liquid on aphids.

- **Use a watering can** rather than a sprinkler or hose — you will use less water.

The average roof collects about 25,000 gallons of rain a year! This could fill 500 rain barrels with free water.

- **Collect the rainwater from your roof** in a rain barrel (or two).

- **Retain moisture in your soil by mulching** around the base of plants. You can make a mulch using organic materials such as manure, hay, or straw, a thin layer of grass cuttings, or locally produced bark or wood chips.

Water is in greatest demand in the heat of summer, when over 50% of home water use can go toward watering gardens.

- **Plant close together** to conserve water in the soil.

- **Choose drought-resistant plants**, flowers, and shrubs that positively enjoy dry, hot conditions, such as evening primrose, buddleia, rockrose, thyme, and lavender.

- **Keep your gutters clear of leaves**.

- **Make compost** (see pages 55–56). Instead of throwing away all your garden waste, vegetable peelings, paper, and cardboard, compost them. You can use the compost to form a layer of mulch on top of the soil, which will keep it cool and help reduce moisture loss. Making compost helps to lock carbon up in your soil, which means less CO_2 emissions, and compost in soil acts like a sponge, holding on to water and nutrients and reducing the need to water and fertilize.

- **Leave the lawn longer** — save on water and leave your mower in the shed!

- **Don't water the lawn** — it will recover when it rains again.

A garden hose or sprinkler can use almost as much water in an hour as an average family of four uses in one day.

LATER . . .

- **Install rain barrels** to collect the rainwater from your roof.

- **Check out a reel mower** — new models are lightweight and easy to use.

- **Consider using "gray water"** — wastewater from baths, the kitchen sink, etc., to water the flowers in your garden, but avoid gray water that has a lot of strong detergents in it, as this might damage your plants.

- **Grow food instead of grass**.

- **Plant vegetables** among your flowers.

- **Plant a tree**.

- **Vegetables such as sweetcorn, fava beans, and green beans** will survive with less watering, although their yields will be smaller.

- **Root crops** such as beets, turnips, and carrots, together with asparagus, are the most drought-resistant, but root crops will become hard and woody if they get too dry.

- **Crops with plenty of leaves**, such as lettuce, peas, runner beans, tomatoes, potatoes, salad onions, cauliflower, and broccoli, require the most water.

- **Summer squashes, zucchinis, and cucumbers** need regular watering once their fruit begins to swell.

- **Don't water your plants little and often**, as this encourages shallow rooting. Do it occasionally but thoroughly, which will make them more resistant to drought.

- **Direct the water to the base of the plants** and give their roots a good soak. A couple of times a week should be sufficient even when the weather is hot.

If you do just one thing:
COLLECT WATER FROM YOUR ROOF IN A RAIN BARREL

RENEWABLE ENERGY AND YOUR HOME

- Renewable energy is energy produced by a source that continually renews itself. Well-known sources are the sun, moving water, wind, and plant materials. This energy can be used for space heating and hot water heating, and to produce electricity for your home.

- By using renewable energy instead of conventional energy sources, you can reduce the amount of CO_2 your household produces. This will reduce your contribution to climate change and save you a considerable amount of money once installed, as most of these energy sources will provide endless free energy, and reduce the impact on your household of gas and electricity price increases.

- Provided you have already taken some basic steps to reduce your energy consumption, there will probably be subsidies available to help you pay for the purchase and installation of a renewable energy system. These subsidies can be quite substantial.

When considering the purchase and installation of a renewable energy system, you need to consider:

- **The suitability of your home** Do you have a south-facing roof or wall? Is your house exposed to the wind?

- **Payback** (the amount of time it takes for the renewable energy system to pay for itself). This varies considerably according to which system you install.

- **Initial cost** Some systems are dramatically cheaper than others to buy and install.

Solar power

- **Energy from the sun** can be used both to provide domestic hot water and to produce electricity for your home. Different technologies are used for each.

To produce domestic hot water

- **Solar heating panels** use the sun's energy to heat domestic hot water. This energy typically reduces your water heating bill by 65% to 75%.

- **Solar heating systems** work in conjunction with your conventional domestic hot water system.

- **Most south-facing roofs, walls, or gardens** are suitable for the installation of solar heating panels.

To produce electricity

- **Photovoltaic (PV) cells** convert sunlight to electricity. Electricity you don't use can be fed into the power grid, thereby reducing your electricity bill. The PV cells can be put on a south-facing roof or wall, provided that it is strong enough to support the additional weight and the cells are not shaded by trees or other buildings.

Small-scale wind turbines

To produce electricity

- **Wind turbines** convert the energy of moving wind into electricity. A new kind of micro-turbine that attaches to your chimney or roof may be the most convenient and practical.

- **The extra electricity produced** by micro wind turbines is fed back into the power grid, thereby reducing your electricity bill. Your house needs an exposed position to make this system suitable for you.

Biomass (biofuels)

To heat your house and hot water

- **Biomass or biofuels** are materials such as wood or straw that grow quickly and can be burned to release heat for space heating and domestic hot water. Biomass is different from all the other renewable energy sources because the fuel generally has to be purchased.

Biomass is a renewable energy source because:

- **The materials are quick to grow**, absorbing CO_2 in the process.

- **The CO_2 released** when it is burned **balances the CO_2** that was absorbed during the growth of the material, effectively making the process carbon-neutral.

- **Wood (in the form of logs or pellets)** is the most commonly used biofuel. It should be burned in an efficient, controllable manner, either in stand-alone stoves or in boilers.

Ground-source heat pumps

To heat your house and hot water

- **Heat pumps take heat from several yards under the ground** (which remains at about 54°F all year round) and use it to heat your house — just like a refrigerator in reverse.

- **They can also be used to warm water** before it enters your domestic hot water heater, thereby saving on energy used. If you want to install a heat pump, you will need sufficient space outside to dig either a trench or a borehole.

- **Heat pumps are very efficient**, although they are run by electricity: for every unit of electricity used to run the heat pump, about four units of heat energy are created.

Small-scale hydro power

To produce electricity

- **If you have a fast-moving stream or river** running near your house, it might be possible to generate electricity from the moving water. Though not the simplest of renewable energy systems to install, hydro systems have the capacity to generate substantial amounts of electricity, which can then be sold to your electricity company.

- **The cost of hydropower systems** varies hugely according to the size of the project, but they can sometimes offer high returns. The potential source of power will need to be assessed before any other steps are taken.

- **Consider forming a community hydro project**, if you think your local river has the potential to generate electricity. There are people operating successful systems who are willing to provide advice.

Energy labels

All new household appliances must display an Energy Guide label. Use these to help you choose the more energy-efficient models and to save you money.

All products are rated on two scales: the first shows you the energy consumption (in kWh/year) compared to similar models, and the second gives you an estimate in dollars of the yearly operating cost based on the national average of the price of electricity. In addition, the Energy Star label on any appliance guarantees it is among the most efficient products in its class.

Refrigerators, freezers, and refrigerator-freezer combinations

The lower the energy-use rating, the less it will cost to run. Refrigerators and freezers are responsible for one-sixth of your electric bill; a new refrigerator uses 60% less energy than a new one did 20 years ago.

Washing machines and clothes dryers

When purchasing these appliances look for the Energy Star–approved models. This label certifies that your washer and dryer are the most energy efficient models available.

Dishwashers

Look for models that allow for "short-wash" cycles and air drying, which uses minimal energy compared to heat drying. An Energy Star–rated dishwasher exceeds the minimum federal standard for efficiency by 13%.

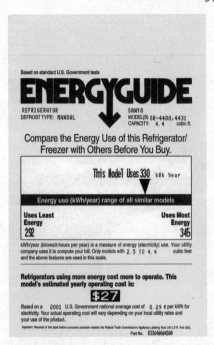

Energy Star® is a joint program of the U.S. Environmental Protection Agency and the U.S. Department of Energy helping us all save money and protect the environment through energy-efficient products and practices.

RESOURCES

The Alliance to Save Energy

The Alliance to Save Energy promotes energy efficiency worldwide to achieve a healthier economy, a cleaner environment, and greater energy security. **www.ase.org**

American Council for an Energy-Efficient Economy

ACEEE is dedicated to advancing energy efficiency as a means of promoting both economic and environmental prosperity. **www.aceee.org**

American Council on Renewable Energy

ACORE works to bring all forms of renewable energy into the American mainstream. **www.acore.org**

Computers with Causes

This international organization recycles computers by sending them to developing countries.
www.computerswithcauses.org/

Consumer Energy Center

The Consumer Energy Center of the California Energy Commission is a comprehensive Web site that will help you choose the appropriate types of appliances for your home. **www.consumerenergycenter.org/home/appliances/**

Department of Energy, Energy Guide, and Energy Star

Energy Guide labels are on all major appliances. Energy Star is a government-backed program that helps businesses and individuals protect the environment through superior energy efficiency. The Energy Efficiency and Renewable Energy (EERE) Web site offers comprehensive information about energy-efficient appliances.
www1.eere.energy.gov/consumer/tips/home_energy.html
www1.eere.energy.gov/consumer/tips/energyguide.html
www.energystar.gov

Earth 911

This Web site has how-to information on how to recycle just about anything. **www.earth911.com/**

Energy Efficient Codes Coalition

The EECC is an energy-efficiency advocacy group working to achieve greater energy efficiency in homes. Read about their "30% solution" at **www.thirtypercentsolution.org/**

The Energy Information Administration

The EIA provides official statistics from the U.S. government about greenhouse gases, climate change, and energy use. **http://www.eia.doe.gov/bookshelf/brochures/greenhouse/Chapter1.htm**

The Forest Stewardship Council

The FSC promotes responsible management of the world's forests. It certifies products manufactured from virgin materials sourced from well-managed forests. **www.fscus.org**

Greener Choices

The Greener Choices Web site (of Consumer Reports) rates appliances, cars, electronics, and other products in terms of their eco-friendliness and includes calculators that can help you save energy, money, and the planet. **http://greenerchoices.org/**

Greenprint

Greenprint is free software that can help you save paper and toner. **www.printgreener.com/**

Green Vehicle Guide

The Environmental Protection Agency sponsors this Web site devoted to helping you choose the most energy-efficient and eco-friendly car. **www.epa.gov/greenvehicles/Index.do;jsessionid=8230862312af236250d6**

How to Compost

This Web site for everybody from beginners to experts covers all aspects of composting, including making compost with **worms. www.howtocompost.org/**

National Do Not Mail List

DirectMail.com offers a free service that will remove your name from mailing lists and reduce the amount of junk mail you receive. Sign up at **www.directmail.com/directory /mail_preference/**

National Motorists Association

The NMA has a listing and reviews of the most fuel-efficient cars. **www.motorists.org/blog/the-16-most-fuel-efficient-new-cars/**

Recycling Facts

This Web site at Oberlin College has all the facts, figures, and sources: **www.oberlin.edu/recycle/facts.html**

Ridesharing

The Rideshare Directory has links to other national ride-sharing sites as well as sites in each state. Rideshare U.S. helps to facilitate carpools in the U.S. and Canada. **www.rideshare-directory.com/** **www.rideshare.us/**

Rocky Mountain Institute

Rocky Mountain Institute is a nonprofit research and educational organization whose mission is to foster the efficient and sustainable use of resources. The Household Energy Efficiency link on their Web site contains nine "Home Energy Briefs" that cover all aspects of making your home more energy efficient. **www.rmi.org/**

Saving Electricity

This comprehensive do-it-yourself guide to saving electricity in your home allows you to calculate your electrical usage, explains the basics of electricity, and discusses everything from rating appliances to alternative energy sources. It also includes a carbon-footprint calculator. **www.michael bluejay.com/electricity/**

Simply Insulate

The Simply Insulate Web site is a good place to get started with answers to questions about how to go about insulating your home. **www.simplyinsulate.com/index.html**

Treehugger.com

This is a resource for going green in all aspects of your life, from health and home to office and transportation and beyond. **www.treehugger.com/**

the politics and practice of sustainable living

CHELSEA GREEN PUBLISHING

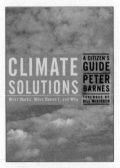

Climate Solutions: A Citizen's Guide
What Works, What Doesn't, and Why
PETER BARNES
Foreword by
BILL MCKIBBEN
978-1-60358-005-2
Paper • $9.95

Climate Solutions explains in clear and simple language what different proposed climate policies will do—and what they won't do. It tells you who's behind the policies, who'd pay for them, and who'd profit. It strips away the spin and tells you the key facts you need to know. In a very real sense, *Climate Solutions* ushers in the next stage of the global-warming debate. In the first stage, we discussed the problem. In the next stage, we must choose solutions.

the politics and practice of sustainable living

THE CHELSEA GREEN GUIDES

CHELSEA GREEN'S NEW *GREEN GUIDES* are perfect tutors for consumers or businesses looking to green-up their knowledge. Each compact, value-priced guide is packed with triple-bottom-line tips that will improve the environment and your finances. Slim enough to fit in a kitchen or desk drawer, you'll return to *The Chelsea Green Guides* frequently for concise, sage advice.

Energy: Use Less – Save More
JON CLIFT and
AMANDA CUTHBERT
9781933392721
$7.95

Water: Use Less — Save More
JON CLIFT and
AMANDA CUTHBERT
9781933392738
$7.95

Reduce, Reuse, Recycle: An Easy Household Guide
NICKY SCOTT
9781933392752
$7.95

Composting: An Easy Household Guide
NICKY SCOTT
9781933392745
$7.95

Greening Your Office
JON CLIFT and
AMANDA CUTHBERT
9781933392998
$7.95

Biking to Work
RORY MCMULLAN
9781933392981
$7.95

To place an order please visit **www.chelseagreen.com**
or call **802.295.6300.**